YOUR KNOWLEDGE HAS VALUE

- We will publish your bachelor's and master's thesis, essays and papers

- Your own eBook and book - sold worldwide in all relevant shops

- Earn money with each sale

Upload your text at www.GRIN.com and publish for free

Bibliographic information published by the German National Library:

The German National Library lists this publication in the National Bibliography; detailed bibliographic data are available on the Internet at http://dnb.dnb.de .

This book is copyright material and must not be copied, reproduced, transferred, distributed, leased, licensed or publicly performed or used in any way except as specifically permitted in writing by the publishers, as allowed under the terms and conditions under which it was purchased or as strictly permitted by applicable copyright law. Any unauthorized distribution or use of this text may be a direct infringement of the author s and publisher s rights and those responsible may be liable in law accordingly.

Imprint:

Copyright © 2014 GRIN Verlag
Print and binding: Books on Demand GmbH, Norderstedt Germany
ISBN: 9783668643826

This book at GRIN:

https://www.grin.com/document/413353

Jobaire Alam

Organizational Identity and Corporate Communication

GRIN Verlag

GRIN - Your knowledge has value

Since its foundation in 1998, GRIN has specialized in publishing academic texts by students, college teachers and other academics as e-book and printed book. The website www.grin.com is an ideal platform for presenting term papers, final papers, scientific essays, dissertations and specialist books.

Visit us on the internet:

http://www.grin.com/

http://www.facebook.com/grincom

http://www.twitter.com/grin_com

UNIVERSITY OF STAVANGER

Faculty of Social Sciences

The Norwegian School of Hotel & Tourism

Organizational Identity and Corporate Communication

Date of submission: December 5th 2014

Introduction

The student with above candidate number determines to work on the assignment 1. According to the requirement of the assignment 1, the writer would like to present definitions of the terms reputation, issue management and crisis communication in relation to organisation. The definitions are reflection of the books and recent journal articles. Then brief and critical discussion will take place to understand the link between these three terms. Therefore, this is going to explore the idea on how an organisation can use issue management to build and maintain its' reputation. Further, the objective of the second part of the assignment is to make a clear understanding of Corporate Social Responsibility (CSR) and various approaches of CSR. Finally, to conclude the assignment, the writer discussed critically the relationship between CSR and Corporate Reputation along with example based on lecture notes and previous empirical studies.

1. Reputation

Barnett, Jermier & Lafferty, 2006 in their definitional landscape article, reviewed about fifty unique sources and defined corporate reputation by clusters of three individuals, such as: awareness, assessment and asset (Barnett, Jermier, & Lafferty, 2006).

Awareness: By the term awareness of as firm, Barnett, Jermier & Lafferty, 2006, mean that, corporate reputation is accumulation of perceptions, latent perceptions, net perceptions, global perceptions, perceptual representations and overall collective representations (Barnett et al., 2006). They farther add, "…references to corporate reputation as representations of knowledge or emotions since these indicate an awareness of the firm."

Assessment: The second cluster is reputation as assessment (Barnett et al., 2006). In the assessment cluster, they include the terms, indicators and languages, which all the stakeholder groups use to assess the status of the organization. In this criterion, they include the references to organizational reputation "as Judgment, an evaluation or a gauge" (Barnett et al., 2006). They suggest adding the term opinion and belief as the definition is as judgmental in nature.

Asset: The authors call asset of the organization as the last cluster of corporate reputation, which is something valuable and particularly significant to the firm (Barnett et al., 2006). In this group, the authors add the references to the term 'as a resource or as an intangible, financial or economic asset.' (Barnett et al., 2006).

Clardy, A. 2012, in the article about organizational reputation agree on these cluster based definition and present a similar definition to elaborate that issues in conceptualize and measurement (Clardy, 2012). The frame of three individuals has a real value for reputation of an organization (Clardy, 2012). The author clarify by explaining that, these clusters may overlap in some situation but they are relatively distinctive, '... awareness doesn't imply an assessment; assessment doesn't imply transformation into asset.' (Clardy, 2012).

Kent Walker, 2010 in the empirical study reveals a systematic review of corporate reputation. Firstly, the author differentiated from the organizational identity and image. Secondly, the evaluation of corporate reputation depend on length (Walker, 2010). Walker mentions about the interconnectedness between the variables of around the corporate reputation. Because, it is important to follow specific definition, then the situation will define the other independent issues, which are influencing corporate reputation (Walker, 2010).

2. Issue Management

First, I would like to mention that, it was not easy to get a specific recent research on the definition of issue management. However, Brad, H. & Max, M. 1989 in their empirical survey study on 'how corporations define issue management' found two elements such as identification of an issue and the influence combined the issue management (Hainsworth & Meng, 1989). If a management can identify an issue beforehand, that may have impact upon organization's operations, then if the management adopt the proper action, thus, there is a perfect influence on the development of the issue (Hainsworth & Meng, 1989). In their survey, respondents of four corporations indicated three aspects to the strategic response, such as, analysis of the position of the organization, strategic plan to influence the issue and implementation with continuous evaluation according to the organizational expectations (Hainsworth & Meng, 1989). The researchers conclude by mentioning that issue management as an action oriented management policy that seeks to '…identify potential or emerging issues …' issues can be '…legislative, regulatory, political, or social...' which has impact the organization "and then mobilizes and coordinates organizational resources to strategically influence the development of those issues. The ultimate goal of issues management should be to shape public policy to the benefit of the organization" (Hainsworth & Meng, 1989).

Robert & Kenneth, 1990 describe about the four significant individuals are necessary for issue management. The four elements are:

1) Smart Planning and Operations: Things which must follow to analyze public policy in the strategic business planning and operations management (Heath & Cousino, 1990).

2) Tough Defense and Smart Offense: Delivering the correct messages to the correct persons or groups with right intention of the affect (Heath & Cousino, 1990).

3) Getting the House in Order: The requirement to achieve the corporate social responsibility (Heath & Cousino, 1990).

4) Scouting the Terrain: The functions which need to discover and make sense of the changing issues (Heath & Cousino, 1990).

3. Crisis Communication

Spence, Lachlan, Griffin, 2007 in the empirical research define crisis as generally particular, unanticipated incident or sequence of events that appears as high level of uncertainty and warnings for high-prioritized goals of organization (Spence, Lachlan, & Griffin, 2007). In this perception, they add the life security and property, more general individual or community too. Therefore, researchers define crisis communication as the target to prevent and reducing the opposite bad outcomes, which arise because of the appeared crisis. Thus, the crisis communication inform the situation in order to encourage the receiver to adopt particular step to save the organization from the damage by creating a rational understanding of the risk factors clearly (Spence et al., 2007).

Meer, Toni, & Joost 2014, in a very recent article on the emotional crisis communication provides a starting points of further exploration for crisis communication by citing many of the previous researches. According to them, crisis communication research mainly handles "…with the relationships between crisis situations, communication strategies and public perceptions" (Coombs & Holladay, 2009) cited by (van der Meer & Verhoeven, 2014) also. As they described crisis plays a very significant part in order to build the reputation of the organisation. However, a bad reputation creates high impact on the all-different stakeholder groups negatively. Thus, the main objective of crisis communication is to deliver the information transparently to the stakeholders to create an appropriate awareness for them (van der Meer & Verhoeven, 2014). Based on Benoit's (1997), as cited by (Coombs, 2006, 2007) in the empirical researches crisis communication theory depends on image restoration theory, which is distinguished in three strategies as deny strategies, diminish strategies and rebuild strategies. In the last two strategies, an organization remarks the crisis, 'but emphasizes that the organization does everything in its power to restore the damage caused by the organization' as also cited in the article of (van der Meer & Verhoeven, 2014).

4. Implementation of all these three together in an organization

According to the above brief discussion, there are clear relationship between organizational reputations, issue management and crisis communication. All three individuals are very important for successful organization. All types of needs and demands of stakeholders are top priority for an organization in the existed crisis period or predicted future crisis. Because, after the appropriate understandings of the demands of the stakeholders, the issue management can identify the situation to take the perfect communication process in order to build up and maintain the organizational reputation (Coombs, 2006, 2007). As it is very vital for an organization to maintain the existing reputation, in the same way, it is very important to realize the approaching impact of any issue and to take right action by continuing a high priority of the whole stakeholder. Moreover, it is very necessary to become successful to recover reputation too (Coombs, 2007).

5. Corporate social responsibility

Alexander, D. 2008 in the article of 37 corporate social responsibility (CSR) definitions analysis mention about many confusing or biased or unbiased definitions of CSR, as it is a challenge to express a satisfactory definition (Dahlsrud, 2008). However, it presents the similarities and differences between the available definitions and find five dimensions to categorize CSR. The dimensions are:

1) Environmental responsibility refers to a cleaner environment, environmental stewardship, natural concerns in business operations etc. (Dahlsrud, 2008).
2) Social dimension refers to the relationship between business and society, which contribute to better society, integrate social concerns in their business operations, compare the full scope of their impact on communities etc. (Dahlsrud, 2008).
3) Economic dimension contribute to the economic development or preserving the profitability (Dahlsrud, 2008).
4) Stakeholder dimension is interaction with the employees, suppliers, customers and communities of the organisation (Dahlsrud, 2008).
5) Voluntariness dimension defines the ethical values, legal obligations etc. of the organisation (Dahlsrud, 2008).

Therefore, corporate social responsibility is depending on overall ethical and socio-economical responsibility of an organization.

6. Different approaches of CSR and the relation to the corporate reputation with an example

Wayne, V., Dirk, M., Manfred, P., Nick, T., 2010, in the chapter A-Z CSR and Alexander, D. 2008, in the empirical research and from the lecture note, the idea of the different approaches of CSR is becoming clear that CSR refers to overall responsibility of an organisation. The lecture note gives the idea that more and more business refer to corporate social responsibility. The concept of CSR has become a lot more use within last ten years in many individual areas of the world. Corporate social responsibility is even relating to the profitability, overall financing, corporate image, corporate brand and corporate reputation (Visser, Matten, Pohl, & Tolhurst, 2010). It is always difficult for specific organisation to measure whether CSR generates a social and economic sustainability for the society. There is a clear trend that, CSR is more and more often referring to business documents. <<Corporate social responsibility is business commitment to contribute to sustainable economic development working with employees, their families, the local community and society to improve their quality of life>> (WBCSD 2000). To full-fil the expectation in the wider society, different conceptions of CSR is there to be good corporate citizen, which is philanthropic expectation. The other expectation is to be ethical, obey the law and to be profitable are necessary (Visser et al., 2010).

The discussion of the chapter 7 and chapter 2 of the book of (Gottschalk, 2011) is cited by several other empirical researches, that is implicitly describing the relation between corporate social responsibility and corporate reputation. Corporate reputation is massively depending on overall corporate social responsibility of an organisation. It is very specific for any organization to perfectly and successfully maintain the socio-economic responsibility towards the society to build up and to maintain its' corporate reputation. No-matter how an organisation build up the reputation over the years by achieving success and being properly responsible to the all group of stakeholders, the reputation may collapse just like that for a very unbiased or tiny wrong decision against small group of society, which may highly influenced by that particular organization. "The export of clothing as a very profitable and highly reputed business in Bangladesh" is a good example of corporate social responsibility and corporate reputation. However, because of recent incidents of the PRIMARK, United Kingdom and many other issues in addition are affecting the reputation over a decade, which is really a clear understanding of the responsibility towards a group of stakeholders of the companies. The issues are such as; work intensive production with a very low salary for the key workers in the garments sector of Bangladesh along with all the other securities of socio-economic life standards. Moreover, there is a huge cost difference between supplier countries and consumer countries, companies are controlling the brand in supply chain to achieve the most of the profit, a very low transparency with an excuse of communication barriers etc.

Conclusion

To conclude, the author would like to add that, reputation is such a valuable medal for an organization that leads a character, integrity, identity and it is able to brings many more and so on. According to the very brief discussion about the links and relationship between the terms above, it is clear that one term cannot exist without the other one. Corporate reputation is depending on CSR, when a bad or good issue approach as a crisis for the organization, the issue management is necessary to be active in order to maintain or recover the reputation in a transparent way of communication. One cannot be without the other one.

Reference

Barnett, Michael L, Jermier, John M, & Lafferty, Barbara A. (2006). Corporate reputation: The definitional landscape. *Corporate Reputation Review, 9*(1), 26-38.

Clardy, Alan. (2012). Organizational reputation: Issues in conceptualization and measurement. *Corporate Reputation Review, 15*(4), 285-303.

Coombs, W Timothy. (2006). The protective powers of crisis response strategies: Managing reputational assets during a crisis. *Journal of Promotion Management, 12*(3-4), 241-260.

Coombs, W Timothy. (2007). Protecting organization reputations during a crisis: The development and application of situational crisis communication theory. *Corporate Reputation Review, 10*(3), 163-176.

Coombs, W Timothy, & Holladay, Sherry J. (2009). Further explorations of post-crisis communication: Effects of media and response strategies on perceptions and intentions. *Public Relations Review, 35*(1), 1-6.

Dahlsrud, Alexander. (2008). How corporate social responsibility is defined: an analysis of 37 definitions. *Corporate social responsibility and environmental management, 15*(1), 1-13.

Gottschalk, Petter. (2011). *Corporate social responsibility, governance and corporate reputation*: World Scientific.

Hainsworth, Brad, & Meng, Max. (1989). How corporations define issue management. *Public Relations Review, 14*(4), 18-30.

Heath, Robert L, & Cousino, Kenneth R. (1990). Issues management: End of first decade progress report. *Public Relations Review, 16*(1), 6-18.

Spence, Patric R, Lachlan, Kenneth A, & Griffin, Donyale R. (2007). Crisis communication, race, and natural disasters. *Journal of Black Studies, 37*(4), 539-554.

van der Meer, Toni GLA, & Verhoeven, Joost WM. (2014). Emotional crisis communication. *Public Relations Review*.

Visser, Wayne, Matten, Dirk, Pohl, Manfred, & Tolhurst, Nick. (2010). *The A to Z of corporate social responsibility*: John Wiley & Sons.

Walker, Kent. (2010). A systematic review of the corporate reputation literature: Definition, measurement, and theory. *Corporate Reputation Review, 12*(4), 357-387.

YOUR KNOWLEDGE HAS VALUE

- We will publish your bachelor's and master's thesis, essays and papers

- Your own eBook and book - sold worldwide in all relevant shops

- Earn money with each sale

Upload your text at www.GRIN.com and publish for free